The Path: 21 Tanka

Dawn Morningstar

BookLeaf Publishing

Presentation by *BookLeaf Publishing*

Web: www.bookleafpub.com

E-mail: info@bookleafpub.com

ISBN: 9789357690959

First edition 2022

DEDICATION

For Jason, who walks with me.

ACKNOWLEDGEMENT

Without a message from Sara Puryear-Dunn, this book would never have happened. Thank you for thinking of me.

In my exploration of tanka, there have been stalwart supporters along my path. With love and affection, I thank Louis Garcia, Gina Razon, Jeanne Clifton, Zoe Lawson, and Barbara Wilson. You are my pillars of strength.

But that list is not complete without Susan Bingham. She has supported me in ways that I am still discovering, and without her gentle guidance, this book would be far less than it is. Thank you for believing in me so much that I believe in myself.

A poet's soul needs tending, and my darling Linda Brown has a knack for knowing just when to check in. Thank you for looking after me.

In my daily tanka practice, I drew inspiration from Lisa Joseph, and am grateful for her example.

I'm also deeply grateful to my student, Dorothy Cypher, whose faith drives me to want to learn and do more.

And my sincere thanks to all those who offered and continue to provide encouragement along the journey. Without your reactions, comments and steady support, I may not have come this far.

PREFACE

I've been writing tanka daily for more than two years and there are several themes that I return to over and over again. So when I was presented with the opportunity to publish a book of 21 poems, I knew the subject almost instantly. "The Path." Mostly the path of artistic creation and expression, but also of accomplishing any goal. I wanted to share tanka inspired by moments I've experience on the journey and through the process, and offer inspiration along the way. I find beauty in the finite nature of creating something and wanted to capture the feeling of mono no aware inherent in it. I invite you along this brief journey, and hope my words help you along your own path.

—

Opportunity
Beautifully presented
Begs to be engaged
Explore possibilities
And throw yourself at the task

The path may be long
And possibly treacherous
But we still press on
Reward awaits up ahead
The journey begins once more

三

Inspiration comes
As fierce as the northern wind
And just as chilling
A cold so deep that it burns
Into the depths of your soul

四

Inspired ideas
Take on a life of their own
Driven by passion
Sustained by dedication
Creativity enflamed

五.

The feeling, fading
Inspiration's fiery glow
Now tempered by time
It is with dedication
And hard work that we succeed

Paralyzed by fear
Whether success or failure
Makes no difference
Pressing on in spite of it
Holds the key to bravery

七つ

A little practice
Can help ease an anxious mind
With a daunting task
Even the smallest step will
Move you forward to your goal

八

Sometimes another's
Brilliance banishes shadows
From your chosen path.
How does one thank the beacon
For her illumination?

九つ

Some days hold failure
Forgotten steps and lost words
Lessons to be learned
Determined not to repeat
The mistakes of yesterday

＋

Interrupted thoughts
Dreams dashed in untold pieces
Blinded by my tears
Each small step, utter torture
And yet I still walk the path.

＋一

Caught in a whirlwind
Overwhelmed by the maelstrom
Lost in dark chaos
Resolute that I will find
A light to guide me back home

十二

At the precipice
While the wind blows strong and fierce
Holding on to hope
Tethered between talent and
Ambition, riding out the storm

十三

Among the ashes
Of quiet expectations
A glimmer of hope
When all else was burned away
This bit of treasure remained

十四

Sometimes we succeed
Sometimes we must start again
Redoubling effort
Focus on the lessons learned
And not the sting of failure

十五

Determination
In the face of great darkness
Searching for the light
Just over the horizon
Opportunity awaits

十六

Taking the next step
Terrifying leap of faith
Even if prepared
Naught to do but take a breath
Keep pressing ever onward

十七

It's the uphill climb
An everyday struggle
To blaze your own path
You must persist, pass through the
Crushing doubt, ever forward.

There is no shame in
Small steps along the journey
The path is the same
Whether the footfalls are fast
Or not is of no matter

十九

When dreams coalesce
And the pieces fall in place
Hard work has prevailed
Shaping the future with joy
Creating reality

二十

Inspiration filled
Now beyond overflowing
The fire rekindled
Possibilities beckon
Wanting to be realized

Anticipation
And anxiety at the
End of this journey
Hesitation as I step
Forward into the unknown